THE EYES DON'T ALWAYS WANT TO STAY OPEN

THE EYES DON'T ALWAYS
WANT TO STAY OPEN

Other Books by Phillip Lopate

Poetry

The Daily Round: New Poems (SUN)

Fiction

In Coyocan (Swollen Magpie Press)

Non-Fiction

Being With Children (Doubleday)

THE EYES
DON'T
ALWAYS WANT
TO
STAY OPEN

Poems and a Japanese Fairy Tale
by Phillip Lopate

SUN

New York 1976

Many of these poems appeared previously in *Mulberry*, *New York Times*, *Telephone*, *Readings at Faux Pas*, *Yale Literary Review*, *New Worlds*, *Penumbra*, *Sundial*, *Sun*, *First Issue*, *Tarzan of the Apes*, *Center*, *Right On*, *The World*, *Seraphim*, *The Herald*, *Broadway Boogie*, *Equal Time*, *West End*. "We Who Are Your Closest Friends" appeared as a broadside edition published by the Cantina Press (Northampton, Mass.).

Design by Leonard Lopate

Photographs by Susan Opotow

ISBN 0-915342-12-X (paperback)
ISBN 0-915342-13-8 (hardcover)

Library of Congress Catalog Card No. 74-34536

Second Edition, newly reset and designed.

The publication of this book is supported by a grant from the National Endowment for the Arts in Washington, D.C., a Federal agency.

To New York City, and to Carol

Contents

Part One

"We who are"	5
Snowball Journal	7
In the Time	13
White Sails	15
She Wishes She Had What She Has	17
Edwardian Dilemmas	18
The House on Castro Street	20
The Eyes Don't Always Want to Stay Open	23
The Horny Couple	24
The Note Left in the Bottle	25
Poem	26
1949	27
Nose Job	29
The Pink Cloud	30
The Ecstasy	32
Split Ends	34
Madonna of the Masseuses	36

Part Two

How the Cloudy Lake Was Formed	39
"Look at the squirrel"	47
To Your Boobs	48
Fedora	49
Petit Mal	51
Walking Backwards	53
Solidarity with Mozambique	55
Satin Doll	57

PART ONE

we who are
your closest friends
feel the time
has come to tell you
that every Thursday
we have been meeting
as a group
to devise ways
to keep you
in perpetual uncertainty
frustration
discontent and
torture
by neither loving you
as much as you want
nor cutting you adrift

your analyst is
in on it
plus your boyfriend
and your ex-husband
and we have pledged
to disappoint you
as long as you need us

in announcing our
association
we realize we have
placed in your hands
a possible antidote
against uncertainty
indeed against ourselves
but since our Thursday nights
have brought us

to a community of purpose
rare in itself
with you as
the natural center
we feel hopeful you
will continue to make
unreasonable
demands for affection
if not as a consequence
of your
disastrous personality
then for the good of the collective

Snowball Journal

to Carol

1.

Our room, says the lady of the house
is nicer than one in a motel
                    and she's right
second-storey bay windows
a mushy double bed   T.V.
and sportsman and gun magazines

2.

We'll take it
But not the meal plan.

3.

It turns out she is an alcoholic

4.

Those circular curtain rods
are a nice personal touch
she must have put a lot of work
                    into this house . . .
we settle down to make love
on a chair
the dependable thrill of foreign rooms, positions
                    violating good people's rugs

5.

I stroke your legs and breasts as you straddle me

6.

We bring out the Polaroid
take pictures of our bodies relaxed
Just lean against the radiator, your back to the sun
a smile of bones dissolving
        I squeeze the knob until it says YES

7.

But you always manage
to take three more pictures of me
than I do of you

8.

We must take a stroll in the woods before the sun goes down
you slip out while I am reading
                and drive to the country store
                bringing back Vermont cheese,
                bread for sandwiches, Utica beer
                and Tasty Cups
                For this I love you

you even get undressed again
so we can both snack in bed
with the crumbs falling between us

9.

We'll never see Vermont this way
up and dressed for our 5 o'clock walk—
the hills above us make us laugh
they're all so pretty!
          and we don't laugh that easily

                    with my arm around your waist
                    it seems child's play to live with you
                    breathe in the electric air
                    what has happened to all our demands
                    don't even think about them
                              if you kiss my left ear lobe
                              and lick the other one
                              I'll be as happy as

10.

The sun is dying on the sharp points of the tree-tops
not just disappearing
soon we'll have to go back to the car, it's
getting cold

11.

I can't resist—I surprise you with a snowball
                    the snow dribbles onto your
                              bare breasts
now you have 'snowy breasts'

12.

Dinner is delicious! We compliment each other
for walking out of that expensive Auberge down the road
and saying no to The Reluctant Panther

This one is moderate but certainly as good as the others!
We listen with delight as people in the next room
                    are being turned away

          Thank goodness we made our reservations just in time!

'Try the banana-loaf bread'
    'I can't believe these lamb chops!'
          greasing our teeth and fingers into the bone

Families of skiers clomp into the dining room
study menus, talking about the slopes
Most have fat asses and need the exercise
But they are ordering everything! lobster with roast beef
          and pie
What could be more fun than eating! they cry
a hearty meal after a long day outdoors
is justice.

          Mother and daughter look-alikes
          That girl could be pretty if she lost fifteen pounds
          Now you know what she'll be like at forty.

13.

At night you fall asleep
and I stay up to read
                    nothing on television

14.

The next day—clouds, a little somber
we wake up leisurely
and dawdle over breakfast in the trucker's diner
          you seem apprehensive
while I play record after record on the jukebox

that morning you came into our room
I was stretched across the double-bed
"Guess what?" you announced—beaming, dramatic—
"I started my period."

      Now you're having second thoughts about it?

      Very well, an honest discussion
            let's take stock of our lives
            by all means, say
            what's on your mind...
            this too is part of vacations

15.

We have found a woods that is really private
Fresh-cut lumber, a carrot smell—
on the ground wood shavings, snow, pine cones
          and animal tracks (deer hooves)
I want to go where it's completely hooded
away from the trail
live like an animal between the spaces of trees

      you are afraid that the ice will crack
      you would go, you say, if you had better boots

      a difference of opinion

We sit cautiously on a pile of snow
What, are you shivering?
like a maniac I reach into your pants
          with chilling fingers
so that you will be warmer
          and you shudder
          at the cheap power I have over you
          to make you sigh

16.

The good mood regained

17.

Looking at the Green Mountains from a roadside promontory
Peru, Vermont—

>   The Woman Thinks:
>
>   This is a place to raise children
>   live correct
>   come to peace with myself
>
>   The Man Thinks:
>
>   perfect landscape
>   of mountains, firs and snow
>   I toss a snowball into the purest fields
>   to see if this is a beauty that mars easily
>   or deserves my worship

18. Coda

When we were standing before the mountains
the sun leaking pools on the snowy fields
the hard quiet of the barn and the owner's house
the watchdog's bark
sky so intense we could only look through a crack in our lids
and yet everything was blue—

how little I've been able to take with me
back one week in the city

In the Time

In the time it takes to eat half an orange
close by on the night table
after making love to our heart's content
when the taste buds are aroused to an incredible pitch

In the time in the underground from Victoria to Earl's Court
Sunday morning on a visit to a friend
In the time from rapping on his basement window
to his slipping on an undershirt, pulling the lightswitch
passing a hand over his face and opening the door

In the time it takes to decide to leave someone
In the time it takes to actually leave her . . .

In the time one eats an apple
hurrying before the skinless meat turns brown
or the air bubbles settle in a glass of water

In the time that it takes a man to fix his dinner
In the time that it takes a woman to fix it

between the neighbor's apartment window and my window
between the neighbor's cat and my cat

In the time that it takes to open the door before the Negro
        doorman gets it
before he understands what I'm doing and reaches forward
        faster than me
and I drop my hand
smile, say Thank you
and in the time it takes to write out his check for Christmas
thinking all the while how I hate this tipping system
and thinking of the arguments for it

In the time that a post-industrial society wakens to the
        possibility of Revolution
and in the time it takes for that hope to evaporate

In the time that a writer pauses between lines, picking his
        teeth
and finally goes to the dictionary

In the time it takes for children to shoot up their hands
and then forget what they were going to say—
or for intuitive intellects to grasp the full meaning
and realize afterwards that they didn't

In the time that I used to walk you down to the river
and lie on your lap
and discuss the new morality
while headlights blinked in the bushes of the Jersey side

In just that time
In just that time
In just that time
would I take my life

White Sails

I dreamt I saw a newsreel of a funeral.
White banquet tables were sailing down the Vltava;
The barges slowly cleared the low stone bridges
Stubbing the water with their lightbulbs.

Ego! Ego! the crowd yelled out
As if the body of Adonis had passed by.
But all I could see were the stuffed cabbage
And glistening corn on the cob

Shivering against two blocks of ice.
Who is it? I asked the spectators
And without an answer I started to cry,
Because the camera was moving so quickly

Along the faces
Lining the banks in their medieval grief;
And nothing is more piercing than a tracking shot
Past millions stiff in devotion or helplessness.

I knew how they felt: in my stomach
Grainy, sealed tight with bottle caps,
Where there's so much weeping, and
Every funeral is a relief.

I started to sail after them; then
The lights went on.
Incredible, I thought—a miraculous document.
But as I turned
To share the audience's love,
I realized that no one else had gotten it
Except for one young woman, way toward the back,
Hair pinned up, a turquoise jumper,

Who kept blowing her nose into a wet kleenex.
"Wasn't that great?" I caught up to her.
She smiled agreement through the shreds of tissue
And I saw who it was, and we both burst into tears!

She Wishes She Had What She Has

She wishes she could be married to her husband
Her tits like fried eggs are burning for him at El Paso Airport
As he touches down she crosses her arms over her chest
To push back the sigh.
The married couple French-kisses, reminding him of the time
       she was sickly thin
And he had to support her in the terminal so that she would
      not faint.

She wishes that if she marries it will be to someone tall dark
      and foreign-looking
From the inside of her Kansas vulva she dreams of a foreign-
      looking intellectual husband
She has one: he fits into the mythology of her desire
As he touches down he sweeps her off her feet
And into complications, wind tunnels, and no security
Other than that she has him to walk with in the streets of
      El Paso.

Still, she wishes that he would arrive soon
His plane is late, and she has been waiting all morning
Close to tears—closer to resentment
Which may turn into the reserved air that Phillip hates
When he expects his joyous greeting, all smiles, all tears,
      all tits
But how long can she hold this hard-on of expectation?

She wishes now that someone who is tall, dark, intellectual
      and foreign-looking will come into the lobby
And she will jump up and kiss him
No matter whether he is her husband or not, just so that he
      seems exactly like her husband
(And many men are like many other men, exactly alike)
And that this one will agree to take her for his wife
As the first one did, and even more than the first one did.
For otherwise, why this separation?

Edwardian Dilemmas

What's this prickling that I feel
     dragging me from a contented sleep?
Your pubic hairs grazing against my ass...
     What am I to make of your belly
nudging me in soft places when
     I had just been dreaming of Allen Ginsberg
sending me a letter, "Phil, I have
     no unused poems for the magazine,
but your stuff is
     terrific! I sincerely admire it,
keep me posted..." And I'm sure he had more
     to say but your lips exhaling on my back
seem different in a way that I,
     trained in the School for Husbands,
can read passing well: that you're
     awake and would like me to be also.

"What? What is it?" I say.
     "Just love," you whisper to yourself,
and: "I love my precious."
     Good; I pat your thigh, hoping
it's all right to take love passively,
     yawn, pull the covers around my head
and start swimming again toward Allen
     who is wearing a witch's hat for *Time*,
someone else's hero now...
     or to any happy vision
let me climb aboard, into the arms
     of naked girls in sailboats, kaleidoscopes

Meanwhile you blow your nose
     and kiss me (apologizing for the noise?
cuddling up? or wanting something?)

In the name of love you are waking me up!
"What's the matter."
    "Phillip, my throat hurts."
"Mm . . . I'm sorry."
    "I really am sick this time . . ."
"Can I get you anything?"
    "Some orange juice?"
"All right." I sit up.
    I am starting to remember the overhanging
worries from teaching in a ghetto school
    to unpublished works to U.S. imperialism.
"Wait, you don't have to bring me orange juice
    it's too much trouble, you'll have to make it . . .
Just bring me an orange." — "No, I'll do it!"
    Am I so incompetent I can't open a can?

I fetch a bathrobe from the closet
    the cat tearing after me, rubbing
his head against my legs
    while I turn the automatic can opener.
Gusts of cold air blow through the window
    of our river-view apartment. The can is
crusted with ice, my hand frozen to the bottom
    as I scoop out the doughy orange compost
with a knife . . . It takes forever.
    I realize I am only doing
what you do for me every day.
    What pitiful meowing! and shivering barefoot
I decide that he too will be fed:
    All will receive food from my hands.

The House on Castro Street

Castro Street as you know
is a street that has a very steep
hill
It used to have trolley cars that ran up and down
but then they changed to buses
and so it was very noisy

The house was on the first floor
but because it was on a hill
when you looked out the front window
you could see very far
and very far down

There was a piece of stained glass in the window
mostly amber and red
and always a lot of light coming into the room
though at night the glass looked black

The living room was beautiful
because it had so much in it
but never seemed cluttered
They played Erik Satie on the record player
and it felt like psilocybin
because everything was very bright
clear and calm at the same time

One of the women who lived there
Michele
collected old things from flea markets and shops
So the two living room couches
which were against the walls
had brightly colored pillows with Romantic little nothing
sayings on them
camp songs and pictures woven into the cloth

My grandfather used to be in the haberdashery
business and he had these same swatches
with pictures of New York City
woven into them

It was surprisingly sunny for San Francisco
because San Francisco is generally foggy
and on the bay
But Castro Street is between the Mission
and Noe Valley
and it's usually warmer there
and not damp

We used to sit in the front room and have breakfast
by the table by the window
and bring things in on trays
and sit at the table and eat looking down
and out at the city

We weren't frightened of heights
because it wasn't that big of a height
just the fact that you were above

Why I was there was because
I went back to convince myself
that I wasn't in love with someone
So I stayed with him for three days in the Haight
before he asked or told me to leave
because he was relating to
another girl, named Michele

So I went to stay with Gail
who lived with Michele on Castro Street
There was Gail and Michele and Gregory
and someone else
whose name I forgot

I never was really part of it
because I only stayed two weeks

Once Michael came to visit me there
and I said 'This is Michele
I assume it's a different Michele'
and he laughed

— as told by Naomi to P.L.

The Eyes Don't Always Want to Stay Open

The eyes don't always want to stay open
Even the lake gets tired of looking
At morning sun
Flashing blindly between trees
Even God must get sick of looking
At U-turns and pizza crusted curbs
On the Upper West Side
Sick of the lovers with their clubfooted mistakes

Her eyes never closed
At night I felt them on my chest
Flinching like an incubated chick
That wants to be born but isn't

Even the angels must sicken from excitement
Titian himself would turn away from Venus
And walk out for a breath of air
Pretending to clean his brushes

Pity the fish who look on at the ocean's horrors
Hovering in seaweed—camouflaged
A poor kind of rest
Not until frogs do eyelids make their entrance
Not until recently did I realize you could
Walk out of a movie

I left her house at 9:30
Her street was lit with summer rain and thunder
The lamps sliced open like pink grapefruit
The bums on the museum steps saluting me
As I sang the song that goes 'Never Again'
Never again would I touch the rounded bannister
Never again search the mailboxes for her name...

The Horny Couple

And sometimes in the evening
a dryness enters like the smoke
that rises from an opened peanut.
The couple is running out of things to say.

The couple is running out of things to say.
The couple is hungry to make new friends:
drawing out acquaintances, giving dinner parties
with too much cheese,
forming mad crushes on another pair,
inviting them over for a pleasant evening
and discussing each of their statements after they leave.

The Imperialist stage of couples.
A four-legged beast
scouring the living rooms for new blood.
They must rediscover the teenage sweat
of getting past Saturday night.

The Note Left in the Bottle

We talked about that time and the children
we were. Constant trips to the bathroom
taking care of each other as a bay
pleases its shoreline. I will
surround you for as long as you are in the water.
Feel my tummy
as I piss into the ocean.

The couples came, the women lazy
and English, buying *calamares*
for their children's lunch.
Mostly then I thought the hus-
bands were handsomer than their
wives. Mostly now I think the
women comelier and more interesting.

At parties you always worked hard
to adjust, no one knew what to think of
the pretty doggie in the snow
so competent to bark. We looked
away at the environment piece
of ships undressing in the harbor
"What, another waterfront strike?"

No place to move. The winter threatens
to sit down. In the beer garden
Breuer explains *la chose genitale*
to Freud who blushes and writes it down
"I have come to the conclusion that
recovery is on the way meanwhile a
line-by-line analysis would help." Studying
the view from Mme. Verlaine's asshole.

Poem

We were lying in bed
where we often told the truth
your breasts for instance never lied
there was an honesty about the hardness
of my penis
or when it lay soft in its daydream

Afternoon is the best time to make love
and afterwards you can
take a long walk
to the Museum, noticing the clouds
reflected in black skyscraper glass
because you might as well notice something

Talk about the justice of the sky
how each sky that is dealt to us seems appropriate

the light in your green eyes catching mine
in our apartment facing the courtyard

On warm days when the air is too shallow
we turn the fan on
we move the chairs around
we go out as sunlight fades into the river
and I see myself in some future bachelorhood
trying to hold the leaves, a white bridge floating
over our tired bodies, our raw cheeks buzzing
from too much knowledge

I see me coming back to this neighborhood
alone, renting a room on the hill
to sit on the Sunday Times
and watch the baby strollers
the joggers, the quiet soda cans
floating up the river
and all my days given over to losing you

1949

If you were as alive as Veronica Lake
1949
in luminous tennis shorts beside the pool
   with hair bobbing over one eye

         you wouldn't need natural foods
         or a wilderness to noodle round

     backstage with forties dolls
     you'd breathe
     the air of Saddhus
     from their crushed kneecaps

and go see Duke Snider twirling his bat in Ebbets Field
   making the catches look easy
               sliding into
        Rita Hayworth with her home run thighs

    falling through the fingers of her long black glove

They gave it all away   it was easy
   giving and easy living

         the gladness of postwar cocaine
      and the crummy roadhouses with Ida Lupino

   pacing back and forth in a green trenchcoat
feeling just like Stendahl
          Nostalgic for the present
                   Billie
Holiday crooning:
      I'm so glad to be unhappy
      I'm so glad to be unhappy

You wouldn't need meditation to be alone
You were so isolated no living thing could
ever reach you
                        Wandering around 14th Street
                        with the amphibious crowds
to end up in a night club

                                        jawing away your vital essence
                        into the ears of second-string Lizabeth Scott

thinking where is Veronica? where's that enigmatic
intelligence   and then the spotlight   landed

        like a flying saucer over her lowcut velvet gown
and she smiled to the orchestra

            who for one moment were snapped out of their
        shoelace nod by her hush of glamour

and the murderers put away their gats
and the plot slithered away
                            like an embarrassed Buick
                            parked on a San Francisco
                            hill in reverse

and she opened her mouth   ,
to sing

I can't remember what
after all I was only seven
and I wanted the violence to continue

Nose Job

When I was a child my mother saved every drawing,
every birthday card, every poem
I ever wrote and put them in a wicker trunk
along with the photo albums
and the tax returns, financial documents and leases.

The trunk was lost years ago
in one of the many dashes my family made
across Brooklyn, in orange U-haul trucks.
Now I don't speak much to my mother:
she's become a big star.
I see her in the subways advertising Levy's Jewish Rye,
pretending to be Italian,
        though she used to call them Guineas.
The latest news is she's getting a nose job.
Imagine, at fifty-three years old!

Do you know what history it takes to build
a nose like my mother's?
how many Jewish kids got punched in the face
on the way home from Hebrew School
until they started developing a Lamarckian
proclivity for bulbous noses?

Before that surgeon comes down with his Cossack sabre
on my mother's nose
in fashionable Leroy Hospital,
I want to take him aside and tell him—
Listen, I have a huge oak desk
retired from the civil service,
with lots of storage space.
I know you have your job to do;
but save me the scraps.

The Pink Cloud

How crazy that just last New Year's Eve
you good friend were trying to console me
smoking grass with Guy Lombardo
the balloon prepared to drop

they put a lowdown blues song
on the phonograph turned off the TV volume
and the irony caved me in

so sad that everything should intersect at once
    when you're stoned
nothing with its clean and private grace
so sad about the brown curtain losing out to the car horn . . .

the room collage cut into me like glass
I was hurt with anything that could make me hurt
wanting that gut-stabbing feeling
like Simon plunging the knife into his mistress 38 times
a dirge of bloody satisfaction

I thought of girls I'd loved on either coast
all getting off with their New Year's dates
12 PM
and you sympathized about women and deception
you sympathized too much

        I want to apologize to you now in a big way
like skywriting. Some days I could
go off with Randolph Scott
and lose myself among the Ute
                    for touching her

but my heart is too womanish
take me back, like the Temptations say
give me your sweet affection
only don't give me your trust
because   I still want everything
you've got and everything anyone else has
all of it
                    intersecting / all at once.

The Ecstasy

You are not me, and I am never you
except for thirty seconds in a year
when ecstasy of coming,
laughing at the same time
or being cruel to know for certain
what the other's feeling
charge some recognition.

Not often when we talk though.
Undressing to the daily logs
of this petty boss, that compliment,
curling our lips at half-announced ambitions.

I tell you this during another night
of living next to you
without having said what was on my mind
or you on yours,
our bodies merely rubbing their fishy smells together.

The feelings keep piling up.
Will I ever find the time to tell you what is inside these trunks?

Maybe it's the fault of our language
but dreams are innocent and pictorial.
Then let our dreams speak for us
side by side, leg over leg,
an electroencephalographic kiss
flashing blue movies from temple
to temple, as we lie gagged in sleep.

Sleep on while I am talking
I am just arranging the curtains
over your naked breasts.
Love doesn't look too closely...

the way kids looked at her in fire drills
the suspicion that her mother dressed her funny
always another's hurt
that you can do nothing about
saving your energy
for that last Humpty-Dumpty job

                      smiling at the stranger on the escalator
                  a little more distinguished, a bit more
              able to pull it off
            with that worldly melancholy that's
        not unattractive

but if you were for once not
to move from her clumsy fingers
taking the sorrow she leaks for your oil

if you were once to stay
to sink into that sorrow

then it would be necessary to confess
that you have also felt worthless, soiled
like damaged goods in an army surplus store
that even the hippies don't want

that you have also felt like
a rubber duck
good for nothing but quacking its mama's name
days and days at a stretch
mindless, abandoned in the tub
wanting to be taken care of
held and covered

Madonna of the Masseuses

You are holding a candle as if
To put the flame in your mouth
You would like to drink something
Really hot because the air conditioning
Is on too strong, inside this purple pyramid
Where they have you giving Latin massages
11 till midnight on the second floor.

When they enter you hand them the guest book
And slap the blue faces
Of those who forget to breathe.

It's in the sauna that everyone relaxes.
The businessman puts on his lace panties
And his scalloped apricot nightgown
While in the corner the film critic
Collects his darkness, through the titles
That are neither film nor life.
And when no one is looking the knife sharpener
Fondles his pumice stone with eyes closed
And the street vendor kneels down
Before his white Sabrett wagon.

Even the family comes to unwind.
The father has his paper and marshmallow cookies
The mother weeping stuffs her mouth with veal
The son plays with his quiet compass
The daughter makes her origami moons.
Because of you we are all contented to sit
Perfectly beautiful in our confinements
Waiting for your understanding fingers
    To touch us everywhere.

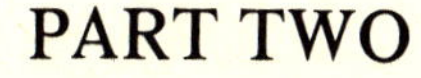

PART TWO

How the Cloudy Lake Was Formed

In the province of Hyoe in the Yuruga Mountains, famous for its cold salty lake, there lived a young woman in the Governor's service named Yukinari who had fallen in love with the Chancellor's son Mei. She was a round-cheeked sunny girl and many suitors came to her family to ask her hand, but Yukinari pleaded with her father to send them away on one pretext or another. Secretly she kept her love for Mei alone. Nothing gave her more pleasure than to see him at festivals riding through the streets in his processional gown. The purple of his court cloak and trousers looked magnificent against the white horse. His brocade sleeves were trimmed with cherry piping; though some thought the color combination a bit unorthodox Yukinari was charmed by its originality. She grew to love every part of his appearance — the fleshy nose, the deep arrogant eyes, the booming chest, even the slightly bowlegged way he walked. Just as sweet pineapple dotes on being mixed with savoury meats, so Yukinari wanted nothing more than to mingle her sauces with mei on her bamboo mat.

But the Chancellor's son had no idea of the emotions he was stirring. He took no more notice of her than of the fleas in his horse's mane. Even so, Yukinari's love grew so huge that it turned into a tree and sprouted right outside the gate in the North Wing.

The tree became very popular with the Governor's wife and was put to many uses, such as being hung with decorations for the Festival of Moon-Gruel and serving children in games with blindfolds. Naturally the townspeople were amazed to see how rapidly the stripling had grown into a tremendous willow oak. The Governor himself sponsored a contest during Poetry-Writing Month for the best verse celebrating the miracle of the tree. All the local wits entered, but first prize was awarded to Krichi, Yukinari's cousin, who had guessed her secret and slyly written:

> *Only yesterday, it seems,*
> *The ground was barren.*
> *Then lightning struck the butterfly*
> *Her sorrow is our shade.*

Everyone thought of Yukinari, since her name meant Lemon Butterfly, while Mei was close to *meijiwara*, the word for electrical storms. Now the truth had come out. Yukinari was relieved, and lived in expectations of an approach from the Chancellor's son. But strangely, none came; for Mei was too busy paying court to the elegant Lady Shinkakai. Around this time a friend told Yukinari that the man she had given her heart to had been seen meeting with Lady Shinkakai underneath the Sacred Bridge at nightfall.

Yukinari waited until the Feast of the Blue Frogs, and as she was serving tea to the dignitaries she let drop from her sleeve a folded note onto the black-lacquered plate of Mei. He put it aside in his robe without thinking anything of it; but that night as he was undressing the note fell from his pocket. It was pale green and had been folded in the shape of a crane. Mei laughed when he saw the queer handwriting and realized the note wasn't even a poem. "Why do you go with that stuckup scarecrow Lady Shinkakai?" Yukinari had written. "What has she got that I haven't got? Come around to the North Gate and I'll show you the love of a woman."

The Chancellor's son laughed and was tempted to take her offer. But on consideration he decided he was too busy. So he took brush in hand and dispatched a reply:

> *My lady's face is whitest damask*
> *But your skin is rather yellow*
> *Like a lemon peel*
> *Left too long in the sun*

Yukinari held the messenger long enough to frame a
reply:

> *The snow on Mount Fuji*
> *Is hard and white*
> *But you should see my breasts!*

The messenger returned and awoke Mei with the note.
He had just gotten comfortably settled under the sheets,
and perhaps because of this inconvenience he answered
impolitely:

> *It's true your breasts are Fuji-like*
> *Compared to my lady's hillocks.*
> *But she has a wondrously tight cavern*
> *While yours I hear could swallow the winds*
> *That blow across the Southern Desert!*

Yukinari was barely able to stand up when she read
the note. She hid her tears from the messenger in her
kimono sleeve. Then she stumbled over to the writing
board and poured out her heart in one last attempt:

> *Pay no attention to gossip-mongers.*
> *No one knows how deep my well runs,*
> *Or how sweet the water is.*
> *But if the lip grows floppy and sad*
> *It is only from waiting sleeplessly for you.*
> *Come my love! Come tonight and drink!*

This time there was no reply at all.

In the days of the Gods-Absent season that followed
Yukinari was too ashamed to appear at court. She
wanted to hide in her room forever. Time and again she
dragged herself to the Sacred Bridge with the intention
of throwing herself into the white swirling stream, but
always a passerby came along or she was distracted

from leaping by her own melancholy thoughts. How could she have loved someone who cared so little about her? What had she done to make him despise her so? Was she indeed ugly, despite what her friends had told her? Had she turned him away with her forwardness? Even as she considered this possibility, she entertained desperate schemes of paying Mei a surprise visit and forcing herself on him.

Yukinari drifted between schemes for getting revenge and hopes of still winning his affection until finally she was so worn out that her health gave way. The Governor's wife was so concerned for her attendant she had her own physicians visit Yukinari's bedside. The serving-girls fed her crushed melon and the Buddhist priests chanted prayers in her behalf, but no one could bring Yukinari back to her old self. Her skin turned yellower, her hair started falling out, and she lost so much weight that she became thin as an old woman.

When the Festival of Moon-Gruel was still a little way off, people began to notice that the willow oak tree had also shrunk to half its normal size—for even a hopeless love shrivels up and dies without anything to feed upon. The townspeople were wondering what to do. A large part of their revenues came from the sales of tickets to visitors who wanted to see the Butterfly Love Tree. Several leading merchants assembled at the teahouse to discuss the problem. They decided to go to the Chancellor's son Mei and interest him in rekindling Yukinari's passion. They found him not at home but in a tavern drinking and cursing the debts he had run up to satisfy Lady Shinkakai's elegant tastes. He was a changed man, broken in spirit, and when they made their proposal he started trembling with excitement.

"How much will I get for this job?" he asked.

"Enough to settle your debts and more," they said. "But you must act quickly, before the Festival is over."

"And what if this girl won't see me?"

"Then you find a way to break down her resistance."

"Good. I will approach her tomorrow night."

The next day Yukinari's serving-girl was alerted to move the sick woman's pad into the front room. The girl told Yukinari she was being moved in order to give her a chance to watch the full moon come up. Yukinari was always very affected by the sight of the full moon and this night especially so. As the moonlight danced over the pond's surface she took up her koto and began playing a mournful song:

> *This world of ours—*
> *To what shall I compare it?*
> *To the white waves behind a boat*
> *That disappear without a trace*
> *As it rows away at dawn.*

Mei hid his coach in the great trees and waited until midnight; then he crept on foot silently across the grove to the North Gate. He paused to admire the dew on the uncut blades of grass. "This is the kind of night one writes poems about," he thought to himself. Hearing the pungent koto music made him so attentive he almost forgot his purpose in being there. He scooped down and picked some gravel and threw it against the teakwood screen.

"Who's there?" called out Yukinari.

Mei came closer. "Only the wind looking for a butterfly to offer his apologies."

Yukinari couldn't believe her ears. Had it been Death come to claim her she would have been less surprised than this unexpected visitor.

"Just a moment!" She was so delighted that she threw open the screen and invited him in, forgetting all her reproaches. As soon as he entered Yukinari hid behind the curtain and set about making tea. Her hair had come undone and she was sure she looked completely ridiculous.

"I wish you would come out from behind there. I've brought you this gift..." said Mei.

"What is it?" she asked.

"You will have to come here and find out."

When Yukinari saw it her heart melted. It was a beautiful robe of richly embroidered light green silk, with a long flowing underrobe of deep red damask.

The merchants stationed outside noticed the oak tree reach its arms into the cool night air.

"May I try it on?"

"Please do."

"I'm afraid it will fall off me, I've gotten so bony!" Yukinari said and ran behind the curtain. When she came out the Chancellor's son was struck with her splendor. He did not even have to feign his admiration.

"You've made my modest gift look like an Empress's treasure."

"Thank you!" she said happily, and the merchants fell over each other with glee as the willow oak stretched its branches even wider.

"How lucky that piece of costume is, to be so close to you," he murmured. Mei drew nearer and, casually fingering the silk as if to identify its weave, he slipped his hand under the sash. Yukinari pulled away in shame, but he had already undone the three fastening pins and the gown shivered to her knees. Before Yukinari could drape herself the Chancellor's son fell on her body and began covering it with a worshiper's kisses.

"Oh why didn't you come sooner?" she said tearfully.

"I was testing your love," answered Mei. "But let's forget all that unhappiness." His kisses redoubled and without any more time he mounted her. Yukinari sucked in her legs, not forgetting how much he valued a tight passage. She wrapped her arms around him, pulling tighter and tighter until the bed began to quiver. Then she pulled tighter still so that the town buildings rattled and the wind shook the leaves in the forest. So absorbed were the lovers that they didn't even hear the sound of a tree nudging its branches against the window. Yukinari was overcome with ardor; Mei had forgotten everything but the joy ahead. Then, just as they were achieving their ecstasy, the oak tree crashed through the walls and buried them under its loving embrace. At the same instant the Chancellor's son unleashed a flow that inundated the countryside and drowned everyone, leaving only the clear green eye of a lake where once there had been a prosperous town.

And that, if you really want to know, is how Lake Yukinari was made with its strangely cloudly waters and its lone oak tree.

"Look at the squirrel
dropping a nut on his foot."

You wanted not to talk about
you or me or us together again,
but to select a point out there.

Out there are paintings, stones,
funny-looking men rolled away from us
like awnings, dreaming androgynous profiles
in trains, the day's delicatessen,
sweat.

I see what you mean.

Do you want to talk about it now?

To Your Boobs

when we break up
as break up we must
leave me your boobs
in a fur-lined box

tell your next lover
as I am a Marxist
all goods should flow
to him that loves them best

but if you won't let them
they'll creep out alone
and visit me at Christmastime

they'll ring my doorbell
looking shy as students
their pink eyes peeking
we were just in the neighborhood—

come in! Nadine and Josephine!
it gives my heart peace
to see such perfect bosoms
floating in space

Fedora

Waiting with me for the crosstown bus
        was a homely Jewish man
                          about fifty-five
      in fedora mittens and overcoat
      and a young girl in a green prep uniform
with golden hair
the kind they used to call 'flaxen'
        I took no notice of her
            busy as I was
      stealing the headlines off the man's newspaper
when suddenly I realized the man and the girl
                      were together
      The man—her father?—waved goodbye
         and stood faithfully on the curb
while I dangled next to her
           busstrap
                in my hooligan leather jacket
but he had eyes only for his daughter
        a fine girl!   a princess!
as classy as any wasp
        And that came from my loins!

      The bus driver engaged the engine
      The daughter's eyes brightened and she waved
but he stood
        hugging the yellow line
               like a stuffed owl

      She seemed embarrassed
      her goodbye grin had hung on for too long
      then I saw her substitute
      a more chiselled smile

the ridge of her cheekbone
quivered
with a subtlety that chained him
as tightly as it now unsprung their glance

The bus pulled us away
the schoolgirl's face turned dull
her color shrank to pussy willow grey
and I lost track of her
among the fresher faces clamoring to be seen

Petit Mal

for David Shapiro

He will be lying in his double bed
Watching the ghost trains flare across the ceiling;
His forehead by the sweating water jug,
His toes in Asia

He is determined to stay up all night
For the illness they have waiting downstairs
In the pantry with the papered shelves,
With the old lady who cooks mushroom soup.

Who will they send up to keep him company?
Petit Mal, the red face who cheats
And cries when he loses? Bully Jaundice,
Pink Eye, Mumps and Measles, or *creepy* Poliomyelitis?

Maybe it's Dyslexia, the crazy rich girl with capped teeth—
Who needs her? Plus her stuckup friend Rubella.
If it must be a girl, just let it be Hemophilia
Or pretty, pretty Scarlet Fever!

He will be lying in his sunken mattress
The pyjama bottom slipping off his waist
Listening to the voices and the hoarse catarrh
The diseases of the phonograph

Mother comes in smelling fresh and perfumed
With green tulle over her titanic breasts
I'm leaving now cookie, she bends over him
And he throws up on her dress

Now comes the time to love being alone
He wants the feeling never to stop
To celebrate the sobs that keep rushing in
Like messengers to the General's tent.

They're gone—some loose skin dangles from
His sweet dehydrated mouth
The rough blanket weeps against his arms
He feels the birth of his strength.

ot saying it would be so simple
ot even saying it would all be worthwhile
mething I do know: the beef would get its intestines back
would get you back
g my hand one more time
  horn of your waist

e would see snow
ing to the empty clouds
guilty wife, covering her husband
cious white kisses to make him forget

Walking Backwards

to Dziga Verto

If time went backwards the bread would
return to the bakeries,
and newspapers to the typewriter keys' chappe
the paper to the tree, crying and holding tight,
the maple syrup shuffling its feet up the bark

Mothers would know their children again:
The rock star, returning with an embarrassed l
would unpack his bag and go into his old room
with the green lamp and homework blotter and
to stare at the ceiling, then see if he can pick up

The walleyed security guard, hallucinating
in the bank, returns to the spot where
his eyeballs first began to pull apart,
like college friends after graduation

The pensive receptionist pretending to look bus
in bed the night before with her jobless boyfrie
the lovers moving from climax to foreplay
from wetness to uncertainty, looking for a sign

The parachutist faltering and stretching his nec
like a turtle, not knowing which way is up

People we thought we had done with
would hit us like boomerangs:
girls walked away from at mixers,
dentists with dirty jokes, gym teachers,
blacks in pale green uniforms
wiping the counter at Chock Full of Nuts.
Rush hour faces recorded for no reason
than the wish that it might draw them back for
this one a bonus, this time for pleasure —

Solidarity with Mozambique

My bank teller offers me a cigarette
and says he's only working at this job
to buy a discotheque.
           In the giddy afternoon
when all else fizzes
        we share a cigarette
we feel creme-colored.

Childhood is over
We recognize each other easier now
like members of a scattered set
of dishes united in a thrift shop
        the nervous habits

digging in noses
fingers stuffed in mouths
to choke back the secret failure

No one can believe that after all
        this sifting through love's shrapnel
we are more than scars.
Old Russian women smile at me in passing
We bring ourselves to nod hello
        while the young wives folding
sheets in the laundromat
stare and stare ahead
at their shadows in the plateglass

        At last we learn to read the world
to walk it openly
        taking love
from the iron of a streetlamp
held in the kindness of those we will never see —

the lighthouse that's brushing
its large unshaven fatherly cheek
                against us
if only we could feel it!

Solidarity with the people lost in office jobs
Solidarity with the red hurt that glows
            from the center of women
Solidarity with the peaceful lines of moviegoers
Solidarity with all those who love the sunlight
            across a red formica table, who take
                their coffee in diners,
        who put away their morning newspaper

Solidarity with the clumsy organizers
Solidarity with the fathers in the park
Solidarity with the ringing in our heads
Solidarity with the bicyclists who wave
Solidarity with Mozambique

Satin Doll

Last Sunday George Soto fell off a roof in East Harlem
Georgie was my student   I don't get it
Some say you were into skag
                                   and in Harlem
ODs have a way of being pushed off the roof

Some say you were flying on acid
           weird ghetto bird
But Enrique the wise argues
'when you're dead
they'll say anything about you
that you fucked your own grandmother'

The Georgie Soto I knew was naturally high
he woke up the class once to tell us
Julio Roldan was found hung in the Tombs
swearing the pigs did it
and the Young Lords have taken over a church

George designs a flag for the revolution
rifles across a field of
Julio Roldan's face

I take some of his classmates on a field trip
                   to Gonzalez Funeral Home
my supervisor worries
           'Make sure they stay the full forty minutes
           Don't let them cut out early.'

                   a ghoul . . .

As soon as I arrive I want to split
OK I've seen it
but the kids crowd around

The family of mourners
retreats before this bunch of rowdy niggers
& sinks into folding chairs
three little Spanish ladies
the size of mosquitoes   chatting
waiting for the music to begin

*

Georgie Soto
        propped up in his coffin
look like a faggot
        on all that white creamy satin
look like a Latin doll on a wedding cake

his plastic face keep changing
                in slow dissolves
first sweet-smiling Puerto Rican proud
then cheek sags onto chin like heavy icing
        the left side floats over to the right side
and he looks real sad now
                        heartsick

                                        moved

watching a great epic movie with tears in his eyes
freshets of sorrows flowing and roaring into the pit
of his casket from hospitals and mothers in housedresses

                                without husbands without money
beating their children in the sepia street lights

as columns of marching hoes right-face
down the hallway, going off and waking
to the aspirin taste of a disappointed suicide
and everyone grieving to the dead son George
who can do nothing about it. . .

he's starting to cry!

     his eyelashes tremble

          you're faking it man

      a white candy dove
      has no idea what's going on
      settling on a branch of orchids
      de Tia y Pelle

       beneath an ozone blue crucifix
       the clock saying he died at ten past ten

if Georgie won't speak up
   Georgie es pato   a faggot!

because only faggots would take that kind of treatment
laid out in a funky wooden box
and once they put you in there you can't get out

dead people are pathetic, man
dead people are   disgusting
they just want attention
dead people are copouts
and need to be set straight
need to be taught a lesson

   but mostly dead people are unreal
strips of linoleum curled in the sun
   jive antique waxworks with no sweat
no heart no blackheads no favorite groups no erections

no more untimely hardons for Georgie
   Yo! Babying women on the corner
     no more Arab bellydances during coffee break
       no more hot fights with teachers
         or fist raised in **OFF THE PIGS** salute
           the motherly white orchids boast to everyone
             How gentle!   How well-behaved!

Georgie all I see is your left side
I want to see the side that hit the ground
bruised and squashed like a battered eggplant
I close my eyes and see you in the box
your yellow cheeks and mustache and black suit
ripped on satin clouds
my guts are churning
you're trying to make me feel bad
but I won't fall for that
I'll look away
I keep looking
this shock is like perfume   the senses deaden
till pretty soon I've forgotten where I am
Skipper notices me scratching my face
                              that junkie's gesture
and covering my eyes
   (I wonder what they think about me now

Florrie signs her name in the condolence book
next to her new friend Mary
and Nelson shakes his head:

             George don't look good. George
             look AWFUL

everybody's down on the mortician

they shouldnta stuck so much powder on him
when I took a breath the powder flew
                    right off his face
they shoulda covered up that bruise more
        that bruise look nasty
and did you see how weird they made his eyes look?

Sweet Pam walks over troubled, whispers
He aint even got no bleeding heart
I'm stunned at her poetic understanding

but it turns out
bleeding heart
is just the term for
an expensive
red floral arrangement

*

Outside I take deep breaths
It's cold and the chestnut man starts a fire
on Lexington Avenue. The check-cashing
is crammed for Thanksgiving
A girl's maxi-coat blows open
and the wind tickles
her great meaty leg

and the last thing I think about is you.

OTHER BOOKS AVAILABLE FROM *SUN*

Love Wounds & Multiple Fractures: Poems, by Carolanne Ely
    ISBN 0-915342-02-2 (paperback).

The Daily Round: New Poems, by Phillip Lopate
    ISBN 0-915342-14-6 (paperback).
    ISBN 0-915342-15-4 (hardcover).

Blue Springs: Poems, by Michael O'Brien
    ISBN 0-915342-06-5 (paperback).
    ISBN 0-915342-09-X (hardcover).

Toujours l'amour: Poems, by Ron Padgett
    ISBN 0-915342-10-3 (paperback).
    ISBN 0-915342-11-1 (hardcover).

How I Wrote Certain of My Books, by Raymond Roussel
Translated from the French, with notes and a bibliography, by
Trevor Winkfield.
    ISBN 0-915342-95-7 (paperback).

Lauds: Poems, by Harvey Shapiro
    ISBN 0-915342-01-4 (paperback).
    ISBN 0-915342-07-3 (hardcover).

Theories of Rain and Other Poems, by Bill Zavatsky
    ISBN 0-915342-03-0 (paperback).
    ISBN 0-915342-08-1 (hardcover).

Address inquiries and catalogue requests to
SUN, 456 Riverside Drive, New York, N.Y. 10027